Contents

Where cheese comes from 3
Inside the Earth 5
What flowers need 7
Types of cat 9
How peanuts grow 11
The first television set 13
Glossary 15
Index 16

Use this book to find out what you know about Science. Decide if each statement is **True** or **False** before you turn the page.

Cheese comes from cows.

The statement on page 3 is **True**

Cows make milk.
Cheese is made
from milk.

It is so cold inside the Earth that everything is frozen.

The statement on page 5 is **False**

It is very hot in the centre of the Earth. It is many times hotter than boiling water.

The centre of the Earth is made from a hard ball of rock called the inner core.

Sunflowers need sunshine.

The statement on page 7 is **True**

The sunshine helps them to grow.
The sun helps all green plants to grow.

The lion is a type of cat.
True or False?

The statement on page 9 is **True**

Lions and pet cats belong to the same group of animals. Lions are sometimes called 'big cats'.

Peanuts grow on trees.
Peanuts
True or False?

The statement on page 11 is **False**

Peanuts grow under the ground.

These peanuts have been dug up and are ready to be picked.

The first television was made out of a biscuit tin.

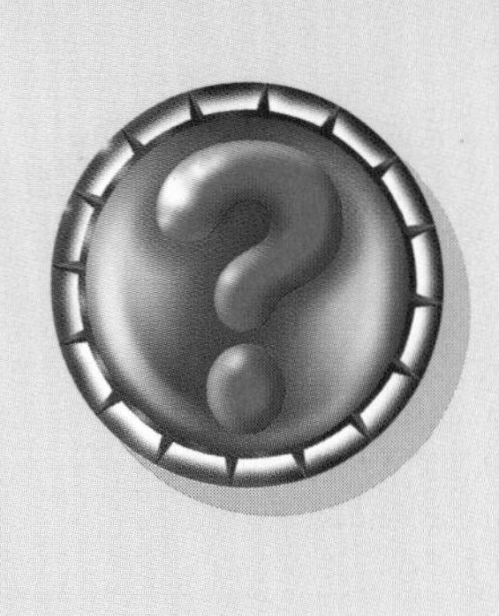

The statement on page 13 is **True**

The inventor used lots of different things. He also used cardboard and knitting needles.

John Logie Baird is the inventor of the television.

Glossary

Big cats

Any of the large cats which are able to roar and which live in the wild, such as tigers, lions, leopards and cheetahs.

Boiling

When liquid turns into vapour; to be very hot.

Earth

The planet we live on.

Frozen

When something becomes ice; to be very cold.

Inventor

A person who is the first to make or think of something.

a
b
c
d
e
f
g
h
i
j
k
l
m
n
o
p
q
r
s
t
u
v
w
x
y
z

Index

animals **10**

biscuit tin **13**
boiling water **6**

cardboard **14**
cat **9, 10**
cheese **3, 4**
cows **3, 4**

Earth **5, 6**

frozen **5**

ground **12**

inner core **6**
inventor **14**

John Logie Baird **14**

knitting needles **14**

lion **9, 10**

milk **4**

peanuts **11, 12**
plants **8**

rock **6**

sun **8**
sunflower **7**
sunshine **7, 8**

television **13, 14**
trees **11**